Success With
Math

SCHOLASTIC

Editor: Ourania Papacharalambous
Cover illustration by Rob McClurkan
Interior design by Mina Chen
Interior illustrations by Pauline Reeves (5, 17, 18, 39, 41); Doug Jones (11, 12)
All other images @ Shutterstock.com

ISBN 978-1-338-79851-7
Scholastic Inc., 557 Broadway, New York, NY 10012
Copyright © 2022 Scholastic Inc.
All rights reserved. Printed in the U.S.A.
First printing, January 2022
1 2 3 4 5 6 7 8 9 10   40   29 28 27 26 25 24 23 22

INTRODUCTION

Parents and teachers alike will find *Scholastic Success With Math* to be a valuable educational tool. It is designed to help students in the third grade improve their math skills. The practice pages incorporate challenging puzzles, inviting games, and picture problems that students are sure to enjoy. On page 4, you will find a list of the key skills covered in the activities throughout this book. Students will practice skills such as basic operations and computations, multiplication, division, fractions, decimals, and much more! They are also challenged to measure length, compare units of measure, identify fractions, and tell time. Remember to praise students for their efforts and successes!

TABLE OF CONTENTS

Grade-Appropriate Skills Covered in Scholastic Success With Math: Grade 3

Interpret whole-number quotients of whole numbers, e.g., interpret 56 ÷ 8 as the number of objects in each share when 56 objects are partitioned equally into 8 shares, or as a number of shares when 56 objects are partitioned into equal shares of 8 objects each.

Use multiplication and division within 100 to solve word problems in situations involving equal groups, arrays, and measurement quantities, e.g., by using drawings and equations with a symbol for the unknown number to represent the problem.

Understand division as an unknown-factor problem. For example, find 32 ÷ 8 by finding the number that makes 32 when multiplied by 8.

Fluently multiply and divide within 100, using strategies such as the relationship between multiplication and division (e.g., knowing that 8 × 5 = 40, one knows 40 ÷ 5 = 8) or properties of operations.

Solve two-step word problems using the four operations.

Use place value understanding to round whole numbers to the nearest 10 or 100.

Multiply one-digit whole numbers by multiples of 10 in the range 10-90 (e.g., 9 × 80, 5 × 60) using strategies based on place value and properties of operations.

Understand a fraction 1/b as the quantity formed by 1 part when a whole is partitioned into b equal parts; understand a fraction a/b as the quantity formed by a parts of size 1/b.

Understand two fractions as equivalent (equal) if they are the same size, or the same point on a number line.

Compare two fractions with the same numerator or the same denominator by reasoning about their size.

Tell and write time to the nearest minute and measure time intervals in minutes. Solve word problems involving addition and subtraction of time intervals in minutes, e.g., by representing the problem on a number line diagram.

Draw a scaled picture graph and a scaled bar graph to represent a data set with several categories. Solve one- and two-step "how many more" and "how many less" problems using information presented in scaled bar graphs.

Generate measurement data by measuring lengths using rulers marked with halves and fourths of an inch.

Understand that shapes in different categories (e.g., rhombuses, rectangles, and others) may share attributes (e.g., having four sides), and that the shared attributes can define a larger category (e.g., quadrilaterals).

Partition shapes into parts with equal areas. Express the area of each part as a unit fraction of the whole.

Cow Code

Where do cows go for entertainment?

Find the corresponding numerals for each number word.
To solve the riddle, find the question number at the bottom of the page. Then, use your answers and the Decoder to fill in the blanks.

Decoder

23	X
17	O
153	E
21	A
370	O
108	S
76	D
9	V
15	F
67	T
22	E
435	P
86	H
88	R
45	I
534	M
118	W
543	N
307	G

1. nine   _____

2. twenty-two   _____

3. seventeen   _____

4. forty-five   _____

5. sixty-seven   _____

6. one hundred eight   _____

7. eighty-six   _____

8. one hundred fifty-three   _____

9. three hundred seventy   _____

10. five hundred thirty-four   _____

TO __ __ __   " __ __ __ " __ __ __ __
   5 7 2   10 3 9   1 4 8 6

Space Chase Place Value

Use strategies to capture creepy space creatures while learning about place value.

Directions

1. Review place value to the hundred thousands place. You will need this knowledge if you want to do well in the Space Chase game.

2. Partner up with a friend or family member. To make your own spinner, spin a paper clip around a pencil placed at the spinner's center. Players should spin to see who goes first, with the higher spin going first. Players then take turns spinning.

3. On each turn, a player spins and lands on a number. The player then says which creepy space creature he or she will capture on that turn. Players write the number they landed on in the blank that corresponds with the place value of the space creature. (For example: In Round 1, Player 1 spins a 5. She decides to capture a Kerpew on this turn. Kerpews represent the ten thousands place. So Player 1 writes a 5 in the ten thousands place of her Round 1 score blanks.) Players record their numbers in the score blanks of the round they are playing.

4. A particular space creature can be captured only once per round. The round ends when both players have captured all six space creatures. Play continues for three rounds. The winner of each round is the player who has written the greater 6-digit number.

You'll Need
For each pair:
- Space Chase Place Value game board (page 7)
- Paper clip
- Pencils

Writing Connection
Describe the strategy you used to play the game and how you think you could improve your score if you played again.

Space Chase Place Value

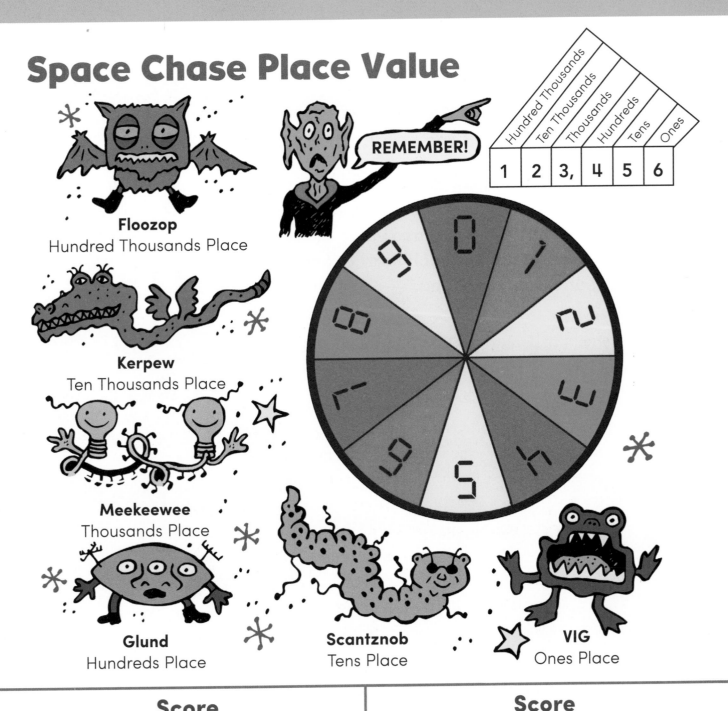

REMEMBER!

Hundred Thousands	Ten Thousands	Thousands	Hundreds	Tens	Ones
1	2	3,	4	5	6

Floozop
Hundred Thousands Place

Kerpew
Ten Thousands Place

Meekeewee
Thousands Place

Glund
Hundreds Place

Scantznob
Tens Place

VIG
Ones Place

Score

Player 1: _____
(Name)

Round 1: ____ ____ ____, ____ ____ ____

Round 2: ____ ____ ____, ____ ____ ____

Round 3: ____ ____ ____, ____ ____ ____

Score

Player 2: _____
(Name)

Round 1: ____ ____ ____, ____ ____ ____

Round 2: ____ ____ ____, ____ ____ ____

Round 3: ____ ____ ____, ____ ____ ____

Place-Value Puzzler

What is too much fun for one, enough for two, and means nothing to three?

Find the answer to this riddle by using place value! Take a look at each number below. One digit in each number is underlined. Circle the word in each line that tells the place value of the underlined number. Write the letters next to each correct answer in the blanks below. The first one is done for you.

1. 15,209   **A** thousands   **I** hundreds
2. 4,729   **N** hundreds   **S** tens
3. 425   **E** hundreds   **O** tens
4. 7,618   **C** tens   **G** ones
5. 1,112   **P** thousands   **R** hundreds
6. 8,636   **A** hundreds   **E** ones
7. 222   **T** tens   **M** ones

$$\underset{1}{\underline{\text{A}}} \quad \underset{2}{\underline{\quad}} \; \underset{3}{\underline{\quad}} \; \underset{4}{\underline{\quad}} \; \underset{5}{\underline{\quad}} \; \underset{6}{\underline{\quad}} \; \underset{7}{\underline{\quad}}$$

Bee Riddle

What did the farmer get when he tried to reach the beehive?

Round each number.
To solve the riddle, find the question number at the bottom of the page. Then, use your answers and the Decoder to fill in the blanks.

1 Round 7 to the nearest ten ＿＿＿

2 Round 23 to the nearest ten ＿＿＿

3 Round 46 to the nearest ten ＿＿＿

4 Round 92 to the nearest ten ＿＿＿

5 Round 203 to the nearest hundred ＿＿＿

6 Round 420 to the nearest hundred ＿＿＿

7 Round 588 to the nearest hundred ＿＿＿

8 Round 312 to the nearest hundred ＿＿＿

9 Round 549 to the nearest hundred ＿＿＿

10 Round 710 to the nearest hundred ＿＿＿

Decoder

400	A
800	W
30	O
10	Y
25	E
500	I
210	J
20	L
40	C
700	U
90	S
100	T
600	G
95	F
50	N
550	V
300	Z
7	H
200	Z

A "B ＿＿ ＿＿ ＿＿ ＿＿ "   ＿＿ ＿＿ ＿＿ ＿＿ ＿＿ ＿＿
      10   5   8   1   4   9   7   3   6   2

Discover Coordinates!

Follow the coordinates to the correct box, then draw the underlined treasures on the treasure map.

C3	A <u>jeweled crown</u> sparkles.
B1	A <u>ruby necklace</u> can be found.
C5	A <u>golden cup</u> awaits you.
D4	An <u>X</u> marks the spot!
A4	A <u>wooden treasure ches</u>t you'll find.
E1	A <u>silvery sword</u> lies here.

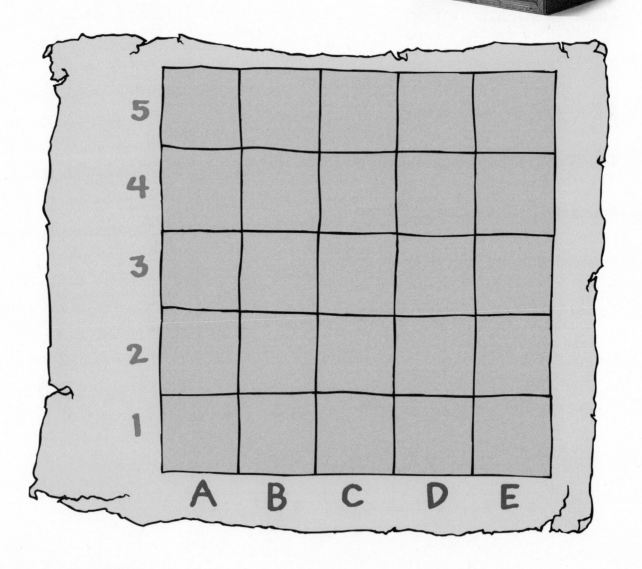

Build It!

Solve the subtraction problems. Then, plot each number pair on the graph. The first one has been done for you. After plotting all the points, connect them in the order they were placed. What do you see?

	Across	Up
1.	10 – 8 = 2	9 – 4 = 5
2.	20 – 18 =	12 – 10 =
3.	15 – 13 =	20 – 20 =
4.	18 – 14 =	13 – 13 =
5.	20 – 12 =	6 – 6 =
6.	12 – 2 =	15 – 15 =
7.	20 – 10 =	8 – 6 =
8.	14 – 4 =	11 – 6 =

	Across	Up
9.	18 – 8 =	13 – 6 =
10.	10 – 2 =	12 – 3 =
11.	14 – 8	20 – 9 =
12.	13 – 9 =	18 – 9
13.	15 – 13 =	20 – 13 =
14.	11 – 7 =	17 – 10 =
15.	17 – 11 =	16 – 9 =
16.	16 – 8 =	14 – 7 =

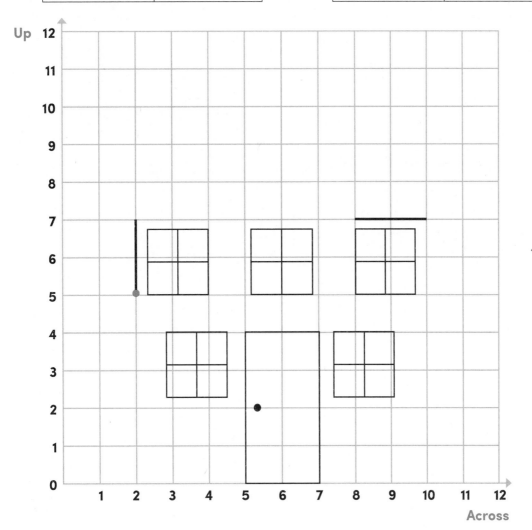

Animal Caller

A bar graph shows information. This bar graph shows the speeds of animals in miles per hour.

**Use the graph to answer the questions.
Which animal is...**

1. The fastest?

_____

2. The slowest?

_____

3. Going 40 mph?

_____

4. 20 mph faster than a cat?

_____

5. How many four-footed animals are listed?

_____

Do the bars show...

1. Animal names and mph? _____

2. Speed or weight? _____

3. Information about tigers? _____

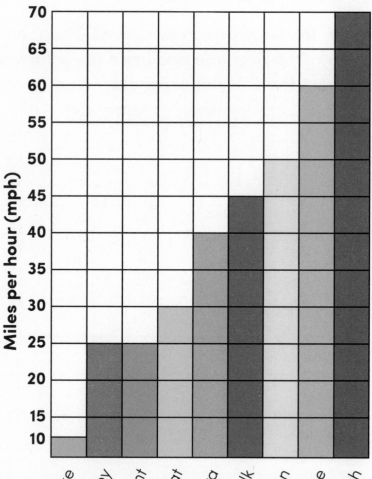

Great Graphing

1 How many pennies equal 5¢? Color in the boxes on the graph to show your answer. How many nickels equal 5¢? Color in the boxes on the graph to show your answer.

Pennies										
Nickels										
	1	2	3	4	5	6	7	8	9	10

2 How many pennies equal 10¢? Color in the boxes on the graph to show your answer. How many nickels equal 10¢? Color in the boxes on the graph to show your answer. How many dimes equal 10¢? Color in the boxes on the graph to show your answer.

Pennies										
Nickels										
Dimes										
	1	2	3	4	5	6	7	8	9	10

3 How many pennies equal 25¢? Color in the boxes on the graph to show your answer. How many nickels equal 25¢? Color in the boxes on the graph to show your answer. How many quarters equal 25¢? Color in the boxes on the graph to show your answer.

Pennies																								
Nickels																								
Quarters																								

1 2 3 4 5 6 7 8 9 10 11 12 13 14 15 16 17 18 19 20 21 22 23 24 25

© Scholastic Inc.

Scholastic Success With Math • Grade 3   **13**

Graph Drafter

A line graph shows how something changes over time. This graph shows temperature changes during a year in New York City.

Use the graph to answer the questions below.

1 Which 2 months were the coldest? _____

2 What was the temperature of the hottest month? _____

3 Which months were 70°? _____

4 Was there any temperature change between Jan. and Feb.? If yes, what was it? _____

5 Did it become colder or warmer in June? _____

6 Did the temperature rise or fall in October? _____

7 Which month is the 5th month? _____

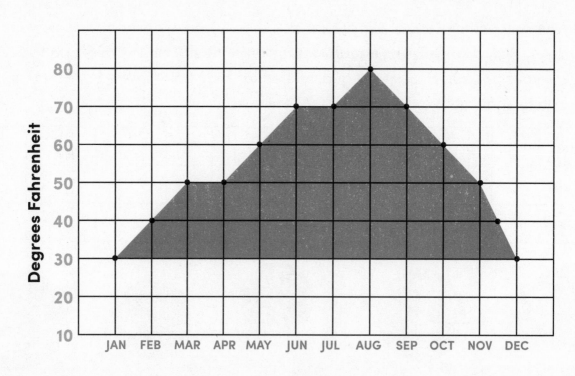

Riddle Subtraction

To find the answers to the riddles, solve the math problems. Write one number on each blank. The first one has been done for you. Then, write the letters under each line in the boxes above that have the same number. When you have filled in all of the boxes with the right letters, you'll find out the answers to the riddles.

What has hands but no feet and runs all day?

1.		2.	3.	4.	5.	6.

$$\begin{array}{r} 60 \\ -\ 34 \\ \hline \mathbf{2\ 6} \end{array}$$
C K

$$\begin{array}{r} 52 \\ -\ 38 \\ \hline \end{array}$$
A O

$$\begin{array}{r} 64 \\ -\ 29 \\ \hline \end{array}$$
L C

Where can you find cards on a ship?

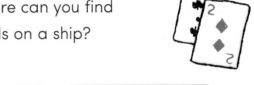

1.	2.		3.	4.	5.	6.

$$\begin{array}{r} 44 \\ -\ 28 \\ \hline \end{array}$$
O K

$$\begin{array}{r} 51 \\ -\ 26 \\ \hline \end{array}$$
N C

$$\begin{array}{r} 70 \\ -\ 36 \\ \hline \end{array}$$
D E

What bird can lift the most weight?

1.		2.	3.	4.	5.	6.

$$\begin{array}{r} 41 \\ -\ 29 \\ \hline \end{array}$$
A C

$$\begin{array}{r} 64 \\ -\ 28 \\ \hline \end{array}$$
R E

$$\begin{array}{r} 81 \\ -\ 36 \\ \hline \end{array}$$
A N

What breaks when you say its name?

1.	2.	3.	4.	5.	6.	E

$$\begin{array}{r} 80 \\ -\ 49 \\ \hline \end{array}$$
L S

$$\begin{array}{r} 91 \\ -\ 49 \\ \hline \end{array}$$
E I

$$\begin{array}{r} 92 \\ -\ 36 \\ \hline \end{array}$$
N C

Eager Achiever

Fill in the missing numbers.

```
  5 [ ] 9          5 [ ] 5
-[ ] 3 [ ]        - 4 6 8
  3 0 4          [ ] 0 [ ]
```

```
  5 [ ] 3          9 [ ][ ]          6 5 3
-[ ] 4 [ ]        - 8 4 1          -[ ] 2 [ ]
  2 2 1          [ ] 4 3            1 [ ] 6
```

```
  3 3 [ ]                            [ ] 3 [ ]
- 2 [ ] 6                           - 4 [ ] 7
[ ] 0 3                               1 1 8
```

They won't let me subtract yet.

```
  7 [ ][ ]        [ ] 8 6            8 5 0
- 2 2 5          - 2 5 [ ]         -[ ][ ][ ]
[ ] 4 3            2 [ ] 9          5 2 6
```

Fishy Twins

All of the fish below look the same. But there are just two that are exactly alike. Can you find them? Check your answer by solving the subtraction problem under each fish. The identical fish have the same answer.

$$\begin{array}{r} 345 \\ -\ 186 \\ \hline \end{array}$$

$$\begin{array}{r} 879 \\ -\ 580 \\ \hline \end{array}$$

$$\begin{array}{r} 635 \\ -\ 241 \\ \hline \end{array}$$

$$\begin{array}{r} 977 \\ -\ 418 \\ \hline \end{array}$$

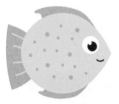

$$\begin{array}{r} 648 \\ -\ 109 \\ \hline \end{array}$$

$$\begin{array}{r} 492 \\ -\ 127 \\ \hline \end{array}$$

$$\begin{array}{r} 628 \\ -\ 329 \\ \hline \end{array}$$

$$\begin{array}{r} 863 \\ -\ 148 \\ \hline \end{array}$$

$$\begin{array}{r} 544 \\ -\ 261 \\ \hline \end{array}$$

$$\begin{array}{r} 860 \\ -\ 732 \\ \hline \end{array}$$

$$\begin{array}{r} 900 \\ -\ 119 \\ \hline \end{array}$$

$$\begin{array}{r} 969 \\ -\ 380 \\ \hline \end{array}$$

Plus & Minus Puzzle

In this cross-number puzzle, your mission is to answer these addition and subtraction problems. So you don't get boxed in, we did the first one for you!

$$\begin{array}{r} 243 \\ -\ 126 \\ \hline 117 \end{array}$$

Across:

A. 243 – 126

C. 96 – 8

E. 105 – 38

F. 18 + 6

G. 65 – 36

H. 43 + 28

I. 234 + 323

K. 53 + 9

L. 84 – 16

N. 134 – 43

O. 80 – 46

Down:

A. 455 – 313

B. 41 + 34

C. 624 + 238

D. 5526 + 3264

H. 169 – 92

I. 39 + 17

J. 600 – 71

L. 41 + 22

M. 65 + 19

Using this grid, create your very own cross-number puzzle. Make up your own addition and subtraction problems. Ask a classmate to complete your puzzle.

Freebie Fun

What does a basketball player never have to pay for?

Multiply.
To solve the riddle, find the question number at the bottom of the page. Then, use your answers and the Key to fill in the blanks.

1 3 x 4 = _____

2 6 x 4 = _____

3 2 x 4 = _____

4 9 x 4 = _____

5 7 x 4 = _____

6 10 x 4 = _____

7 8 x 4 = _____

8 13 x 4 = _____

9 1 x 4 = _____

10 12 x 4 = _____

Key

11 I	48 .... R	23 .... G
24 .... E	40 .... A	32 .... W
36 .... H	52 .... F	4 .... E
28 .... R	7 .... N	50 .... D
12 .... T	8 .... O	22 C

___ " ___ ___ ___ ___ "   ___ ___ ___ ___ ___
6   8   5   2   9   1   4   10   3   7

Fall Is in the Air!

Crunch, crunch, crunch! Do the multiplication problems; then, follow the path of leaves to the haystack. Move one leaf at a time in any direction except diagonally. You can only step on leaves that contain odd-numbered answers. Draw a line to show your path.

© Scholastic Inc.

Solve the Riddle

Solve the problems. Then, use the code to answer the riddle below.

7 x 8 E	8 x 0 D	7 x 5 A	8 x 8 T
7 x 3 O	8 x 4 R	7 x 6 T	8 x 3 S
8 x 1 A	7 x 0 I	8 x 6 P	7 x 2 N

What begins with t is filled with t and ends with t?

35	64	56	8	48	21	42

Designer Diamond

Solve the problems.
Color the picture.
Use the color key below.

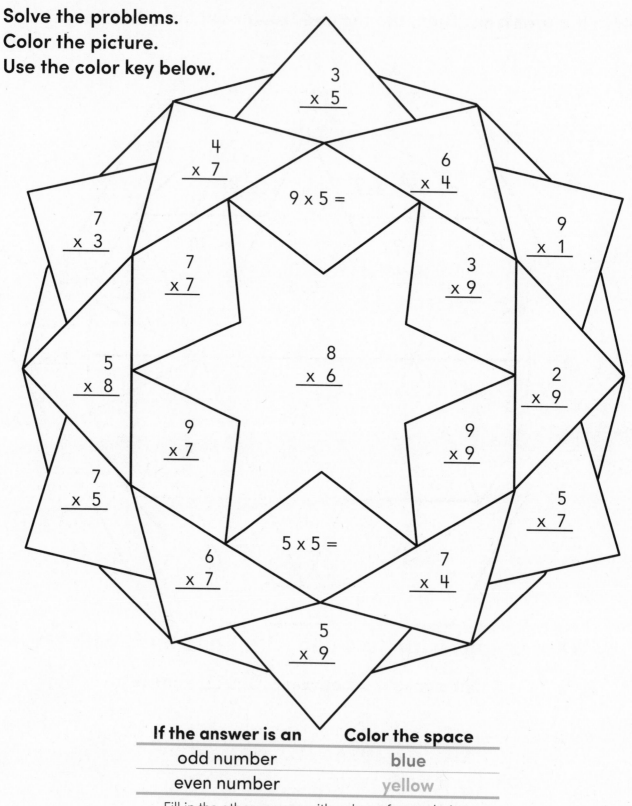

If the answer is an	Color the space
odd number	blue
even number	yellow

Fill in the other spaces with colors of your choice.

Double Triangle

Solve the problems. Color the picture. Use the color key below.

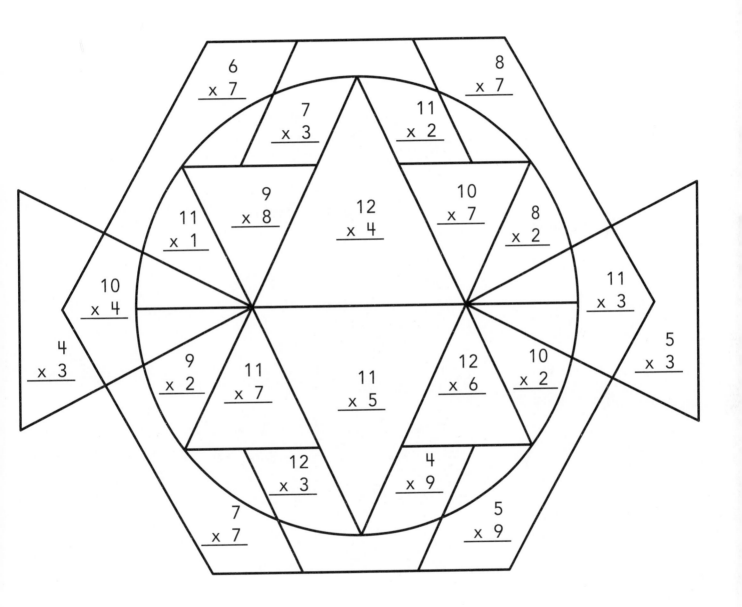

If the answer is between	Color the space
1 and 20	green
21 and 40	red
41 and 60	yellow
61 and 80	black

Fill in the other spaces with colors of your choice.

Eager Seeker

Divide the objects and food equally among the groups of people shown below. How many will each person receive? How much will be left over?

Item	Number of people	Each	Left over
1 28 marbles			
2 15 sticks of bubble gum			
3 8 one-dollar bills			
4 15 slices of pizza			
5 4 balloons			
6 25 marshmallows			
7 6 toy dinosaurs			
8 29 french fries			
9 12 strawberries			
10 19 cookies			

Cube It!

Solve the problems. Color the picture. Use the color key below.

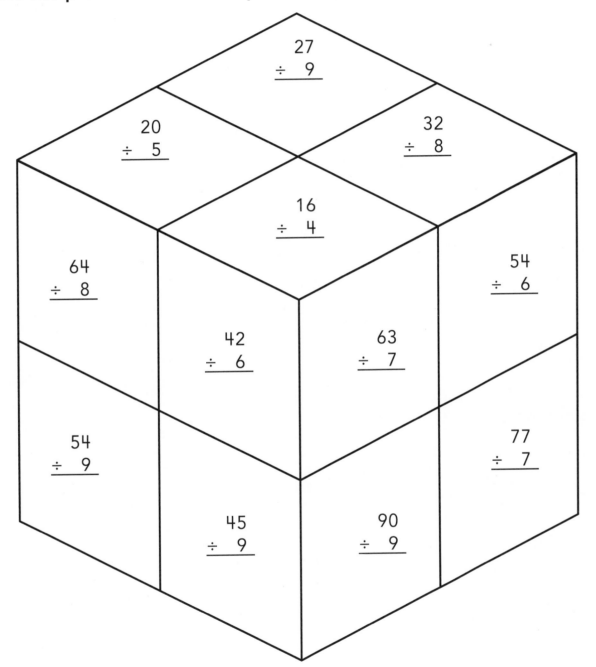

If the answer is between	Color the space
1 and 4	yellow
5 and 8	green
9 and 12	red

Recycling Bins

Solve the problems. Write **PAPER** on the bins with odd answers.
Color them green. Write **CANS/BOTTLES** on the bins with even answers.
Color them blue.

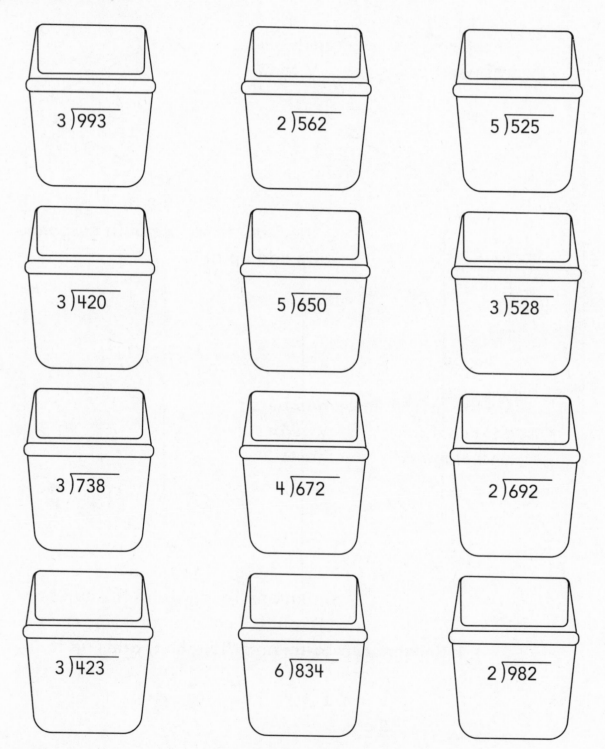

$3\overline{)993}$ $2\overline{)562}$ $5\overline{)525}$

$3\overline{)420}$ $5\overline{)650}$ $3\overline{)528}$

$3\overline{)738}$ $4\overline{)672}$ $2\overline{)692}$

$3\overline{)423}$ $6\overline{)834}$ $2\overline{)982}$

Mathemagician

Write the numbers 1, 2, 5, and 8 in the 4 boxes so that each row across and down adds up to 13.

1

	4	
3	▓	7
	6	

2

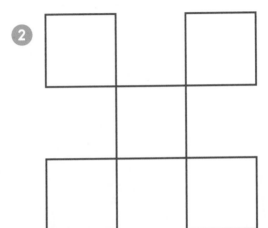

Write the numbers 1, 3, 5, 7, and 9 in the 5 boxes so that both diagonal rows add up to 15.

Complete the grid with the numbers 3 through 11 so that each row across, down, and diagonally adds up to 21.

3

	11	4
5		
	3	

4

8	3	
		9
6		

Complete the grid with the numbers 1 through 7 so that each row across, down, and diagonally adds up to 15.

Who's Got the Button?

Figure it out!

1. If a button is lost every 3 seconds, how many buttons are lost in 60 seconds?

_____

2. Ant Betty finds some buttons. She gives 7 buttons to each of her 8 nieces. How many buttons did she find? _____

3. Molly Mouse organizes 6 groups of mice to look for lost buttons. Each group has 5 mice. How many mice are there in all? _____

4. One group of mice finds many buttons and they put them into 9 bags. Each bag contains 14 buttons. How many buttons did the mice find? _____

5. A second group of mice collects 20 bags containing a total of 160 buttons. Each bag contains the same number of buttons. How many buttons are in each bag? _____

Solve Problems

1 Tricky Triangles

How many triangles can you find in this shape?

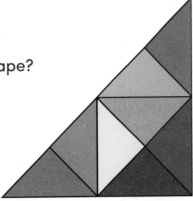

2 Time After Time

How are the clocks the same?
How are they different?

3 Half Again

Draw the missing half
of each shape.

4 A Code for You!

ABC	DEF	GHI	JKL	MNO	PQR	STU	VWX	YZ
1	2	3	4	5	6	7	8	9

Use the code. Write your name. Then add to find the value of all the letters in your name.

Name _____ Value _____

Find the value of some other words you know.

Brain Power!

Put on your thinking cap to solve these problems!

1 **How Many Students?**

Estimate the number of students in your school. How did you do it?

_____

2 **Upside Down**

What two-digit number reads the same upside down as it does right side up?

_____

3 **Cats in Line**

One cat walked in front of two cats. One cat walked behind two cats. One cat walked between two cats. How many cats were there? (Hint: Draw a picture!)

_____

4 **Number Pattern**

Here are the first five figures in a pattern. Draw the next figure.

5 **Cutting the Cake!**

What is the fewest number of cuts you could make to cut a cake into six slices? (Hint: Draw a picture!)

_____

Flag Wagger

Write a fraction for the section of the flag next to the arrow.

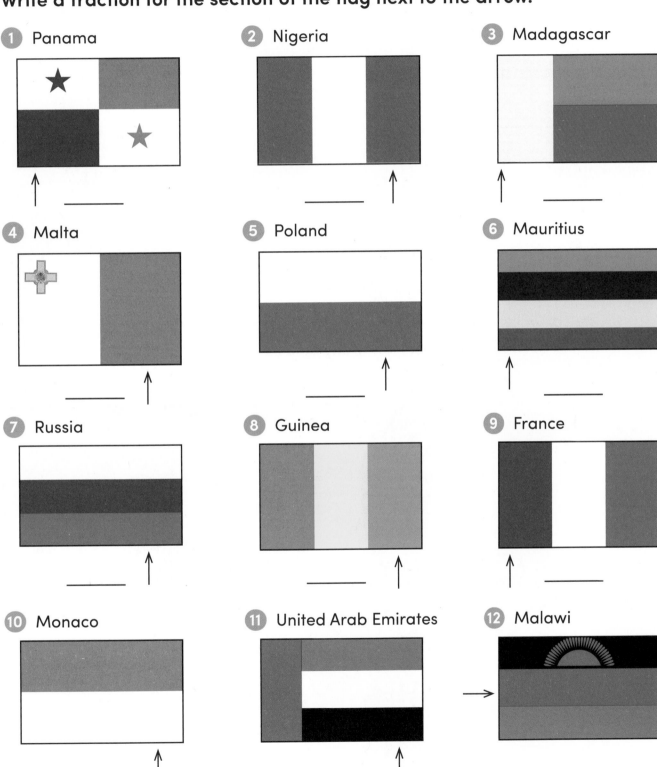

1 Panama

_____

2 Nigeria

_____

3 Madagascar

_____

4 Malta

_____

5 Poland

_____

6 Mauritius

_____

7 Russia

_____

8 Guinea

_____

9 France

_____

10 Monaco

_____

11 United Arab Emirates

_____

12 Malawi

_____

Flower Shop Fractions

Choose two colors for each bunch of flowers. Color some
of the flowers one color. Color the rest of the flowers
the other color. Write a fraction to tell how many
flowers there are of each color.

1 —— are
   8

   —— are
   8

2 —— are
   6

   —— are
   6

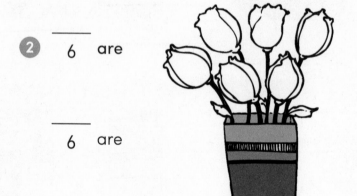

3 —— are
   5

   —— are
   5

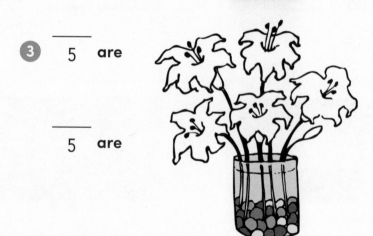

More, Less, or Equal?

Color the design. Use the color key below.

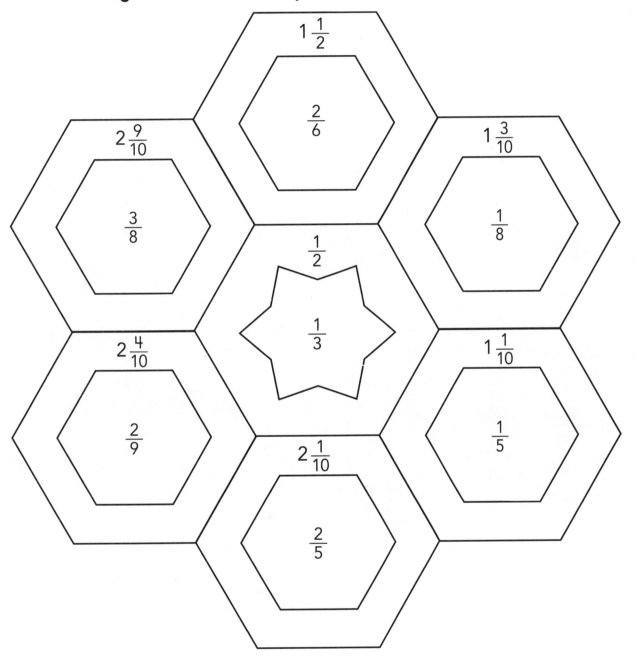

If the fraction is	Color the space
$> \frac{1}{2}$	blue
$= \frac{1}{2}$	purple
$< \frac{1}{2}$	green

Put the Brakes on Math Mistakes!

Take a look at the signs on Bob's store. Circle any mistakes you see. Then, fix the mistakes so that the signs are correct. Now, see if you can find the extra mistake!

Dollar Scholar

How many ways can you make a dollar?

Write the number of coins you will need.

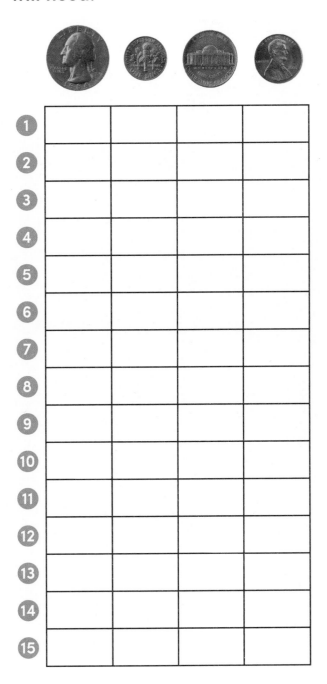

1			
2			
3			
4			
5			
6			
7			
8			
9			
10			
11			
12			
13			
14			
15			

Show 63¢ four ways.

16 _____   _____   _____

17 _____   _____   _____

18 _____   _____   _____

19 _____   _____   _____

Time for a Riddle!

Read the riddle. To find the answer, find the clockface that matches the time written under each blank line. Then, write the letter under that clockface on the blank line.

What did the little hand on
the clock say to the big hand?

___	___	___	___		___	___	___
10:00	3:30	3:30	6:05		2:25	3:45	6:15

___	___		___	___	___	___ !
4:45	6:05		2:55	3:45	3:45	2:55

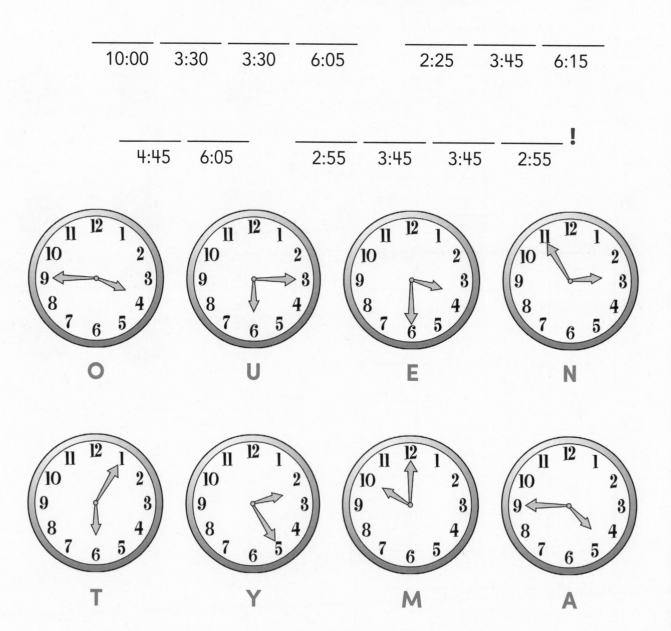

O   U   E   N

T   Y   M   A

Curves Ahead!

How long is each curved line? Guess. Then, check by measuring.

1 My guess _____

Actual length _____

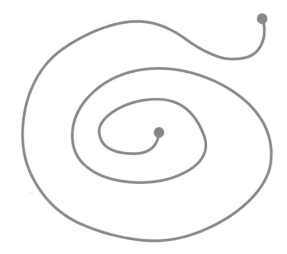

2 My guess _____

Actual length _____

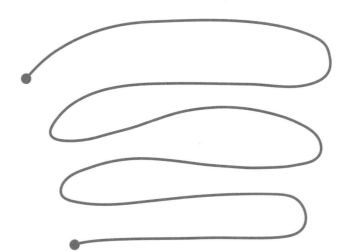

3 My guess _____

Actual length _____

4 My guess _____

Actual length _____

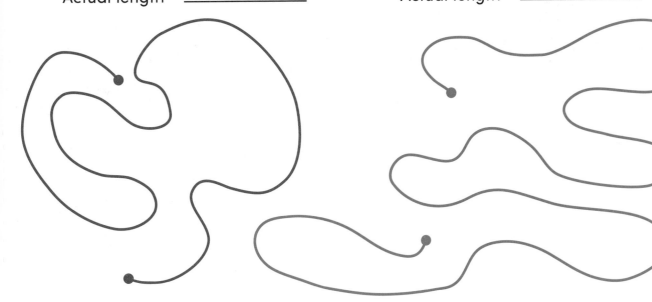

Measure With Me

Cut a piece of string or yarn that is equal to your height. Measure each object below in your home and check the correct box.

Object	Longer than my string	Shorter than my string	The same as my string
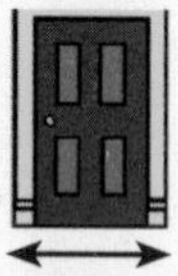			

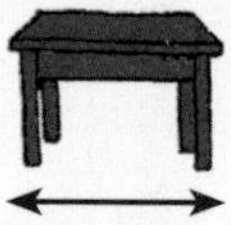			

Measure something else. Draw a picture of it on another sheet of paper. Write a sentence to show what you found out.

_____

_____

Have someone measure you.

Who measured you? _____

How tall are you? _____

What Does It Weigh?

Weight can be measured in ounces (oz.) and pounds (lb.). 16 oz. = 1 lb.
Which unit of measure would you use to weigh the items below?
Underline the more sensible measure.

1 An apple

    ounces   pounds

2 A pair of sneakers

    ounces   pounds

3 A bar of soap

    ounces   pounds

4 A bicycle

    ounces   pounds

5 A watermelon

    ounces   pounds

6 A baseball player

    ounces   pounds

7 A balloon

    ounces   pounds

8 A jam sandwich

    ounces   pounds

9 A baseball bat

    ounces   pounds

10 A pair of socks

    ounces   pounds

11 A slice of pizza

    ounces   pounds

12 A full backpack

    ounces   pounds

13 A large dog

    ounces   pounds

14 A loaf of bread

    ounces   pounds

15 A paintbrush

    ounces   pounds

Degree Overseer

Temperature is measured in degrees. Fahrenheit (°F) is a common measure. Celsius (°C) is a metric measure. Circle the more sensible temperature in which to do the activities below.

1. Bake a cake: 90°F   50°F

2. Ice skate: 0°C   30°C

3. Go to beach: 60°C   30°C

4. Rake leaves: 55°F   75°F

5. Build a snowman: 30°F   50°F

6. Drink hot cocoa: 75°F   40°F

7. Study in school: 68°F   40°F

8. Fly a kite: 40°C   20°C

9. Drink cold juice: 75°F   25°F

10. Eat ice cream: 30°F   80°F

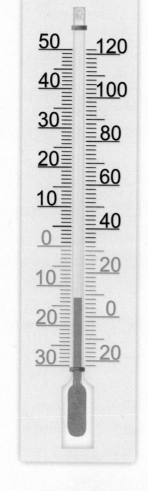

Fact Finder

Numbers can be used to count and to measure. Complete the measures below by writing how many are in each.

1 _____ pennies in a dollar

2 _____ days in a week

3 _____ inches in a yard

4 _____ days in a year

5 _____ minutes in an hour

6 _____ hours on a clock

7 _____ eggs in a dozen

8 _____ quarts in a gallon

9 _____ letters in our alphabet

10 _____ nickels in a dollar

11 _____ ounces in a pound

12 _____ weeks in a year

13 _____ vowels in our alphabet

14 _____ cups in a pint

15 _____ hours in a day

Amount Counter

How many triangles and squares can you count in these geometric figures?

1 _____ triangles

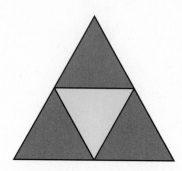

2 _____ triangles

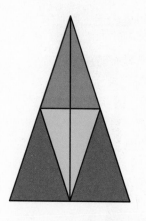

3 _____ squares

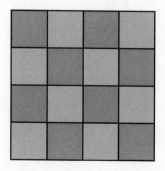

4 _____ triangles

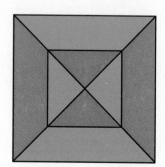

5 _____ triangles

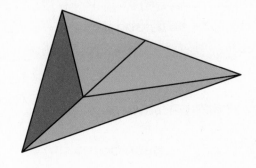

6 _____ squares

Shape Gaper

Flat shapes have length and width.

A Square   **B** Circle   **C** Rectangle   **D** Triangle

Solid shapes have length and width and depth.

E Cube   **F** Sphere   **G** Cylinder   **H** Cone   **I** Rectangular prism   **J** Pyramid

Match the shapes with these objects. Use the letters above.

1. _____ Wastebasket
2. _____ Ring
3. _____ Postage stamp
4. _____ Crayon box
5. _____ Ice cube
6. _____ Envelope
7. _____ An orange
8. _____ A building
9. _____ Fishbowl
10. _____ Child's block

11. _____ Cereal box
12. _____ Planet Earth
13. _____ Stick of butter
14. _____ Road sign
15. _____ Flag
16. _____ Sheet of paper
17. _____ Soup can
18. _____ Poster
19. _____ Baseball
20. _____ A dime

Riddle Teller

Read the riddle. Then, draw the shape it describes.

1 I have 3 sides and 3 corners. One of my corners is at the top.

2 I have no corners. One half of me is like the other half.

3 I have 4 corners and 4 sides. You can draw me by joining 2 triangles.

4 I have 5 sides and 5 corners. Draw a square and a triangle together.

5 I am not a square, but I have 4 sides and 4 corners.

6 I have 4 sides and 4 corners. My 2 opposite sides are slanted.

Terrific Tessellations

What do math and art have in common? Everything—if you're making tessellations!

A tessellation (tess-uh-LAY-shun) is a design made of shapes that fit together like puzzle pieces. People use tessellations to decorate walls and floors, and even works of art.

This sidewalk is formed from rectangles.

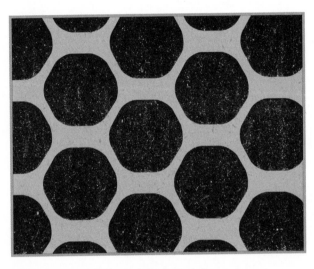

Hexagons form this beehive.

Here is a tessellation made from more than one shape.

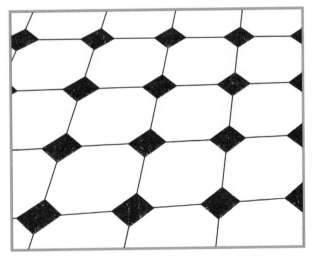

Squares and octagons form a tile floor.

Terrific Tessellations

Here's how you can make your own tessellation.

You Need:
• heavy paper
• scissors
• tape
• crayons

1 Start with a simple shape like a square. (Cut your shape from the heavy paper.) Cut a piece out of side A . . .

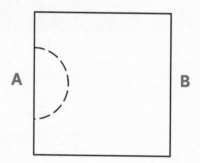

2 . . . and slide it over to side B. Make sure it lines up evenly with the cutout side, or your tessellation won't work. Tape it in place on side B.

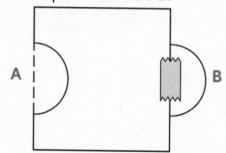

3 If you like, do the same thing with sides C and D. Now you have a new shape.

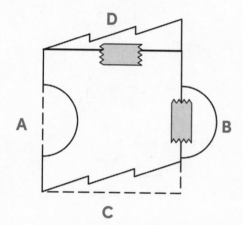

4 Trace your new shape on paper. Then slide the shape so it fits together with the one you just traced. Trace it again. Keep on sliding and tracing until your page is filled. Decorate your tessellation.

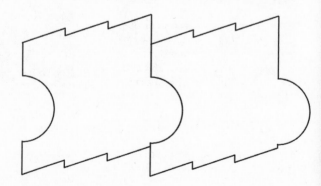

ANSWER KEY

Page 5
1. 9 **2.** 22 **3.** 17 **4.** 45 **5.** 67 **6.** 108
7. 86 **8.** 153 **9.** 370 **10.** 534
TO THE "MOO"VIES

Pages 6-7
Scores will vary.

Page 8
1. thousands **2.** tens **3.** hundreds
4. tens **5.** hundreds **6.** ones **7.** tens
A SECRET

Page 9
1. 10 **2.** 20 **3.** 50 **4.** 90 **5.** 20 **6.** 400
7. 600 **8.** 300 **9.** 500 **10.** 700
A "BUZZY" SIGNAL

Page 10
Check student's work.

Page 11
2. 2, 2 **3.** 2, 0 **4.** 4, 0 **5.** 8, 0
6. 10, 0 **7.** 10, 2 **8.** 10, 5 **9.** 10, 7
10. 8, 9 **11.** 6, 11 **12.** 4, 9 **13.** 2, 7
14. 4, 7 **15.** 6, 7 **16.** 8, 7

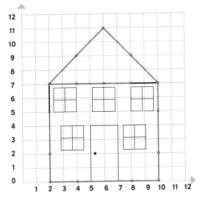

Page 12
1. cheetah **2.** black mamba snake
3. zebra **4.** lion **5.** 7
1. yes **2.** speed **3.** no

Page 13
1. 5 pennies = 5 cents, one nickel
= 5 cents **2.** 10 pennies = 10 cents,
2 nickels = 10 cents, one dime =
10 cents **3.** 25 pennies = 25 cents,
5 nickels = 25 cents, one quarter =
25 cents

Page 14
1. January and December
2. 80° **3.** June, July, and September
4. Yes, 10° **5.** Warmer **6.** Fall **7.** May

Page 15
A CLOCK, 60 – 34 = 26, 52 – 38 = 14,
64 – 29 = 35
ON DECK, 44 – 28 = 16, 51 – 26 = 25,
70 – 36 = 34
A CRANE, 41 – 29 = 12, 64 – 28 = 36,
81 – 36 = 45
SILENCE, 80 – 49 = 31, 91 – 49 = 42,
92 – 36 = 56

Page 16

Page 17
345 – 186 = 159, 879 – 580 = 299,
635 – 241 = 394,
977 – 418 = 559, 648 – 109 = 539,
492 – 127 = 365,
628 – 329 = 299, 863 – 148 = 715,
544 – 261 = 283,
860 – 732 = 128, 900 – 119 = 781,
969 – 380 = 589

Page 18

Page 19
1. 12 **2.** 24 **3.** 8 **4.** 36 **5.** 28
6. 40 **7.** 32 **8.** 52 **9.** 4 **10.** 48
A "FREE" THROW

Page 20

Page 21
7 x 8 = 56, 8 x 0 = 0, 7 x 5 = 35,
8 x 8 = 64, 7 x 3 = 21, 8 x 4 = 32,
7 x 6 = 42, 8 x 3 = 24, 8 x 1 = 8,
7 x 0 = 0, 8 x 6 = 48, 7 x 2 = 14
A TEAPOT

Page 22

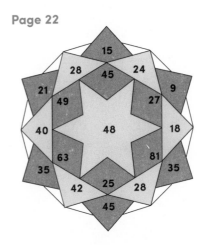

Page 23

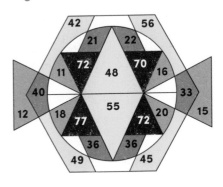

Page 24
1. 9R1 **2.** 3R3 **3.** 4R0 **4.** 5R0 **5.** 2R0
6. 6R1 **7.** 3R0 **8.** 9R2 **9.** 6R0 **10.** 4R3

Page 25

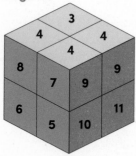

Page 26
993 ÷ 3 = 331, 562 ÷ 2 = 281,
525 ÷ 5 = 105, 420 ÷ 3 = 140,
650 ÷ 5 = 130, 528 ÷ 3 = 176,
738 ÷ 3 = 246, 672 ÷ 4 = 168,
692 ÷ 2 = 346, 423 ÷ 3 = 141,
834 ÷ 6 = 139, 982 ÷ 2 = 491

Page 27

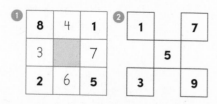

Page 28
1. 20 buttons 2. 56 buttons
3. 30 mice 4. 126 buttons
5. 8 buttons

Page 29
1. 17 triangles 2. They show the
same time in different ways.
3. Student should complete the
shapes. 4. Answers will vary.

Page 30
1. Answers will vary. Student may
take an average class size of 30
students and multiply 30 by the
number of classes in the school.
2. Answers include: 11, 88, 69, and 96
3. 3 cats
4.

5. three cuts

Page 31
1. 1/4 2. 1/3 3. 1/3 4. 1/2 5. 1/2
6. 1/4 7. 1/3 8. 1/3 9. 1/3 10. 1/2
11. 1/4 12. 1/3

Page 32
Answers will vary.

Page 33

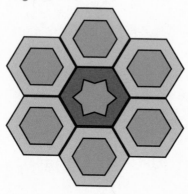

Page 34
Check that students have fixed the
mistakes with reasonable corrections.
Mistakes: 8 days a week should be
7; 8:75 pm is not possible; $10.99 off
mountain bikes; bicycle chain is
$6.00 a foot; bike helmets are $14.99;
you save only $.01, not $1.00, on 2
rolls of tape; free stickers can't be
10 cents each; half-price bicycle
seats should be $8.50.
The additional mistake: a clock with
three hands.

Page 35

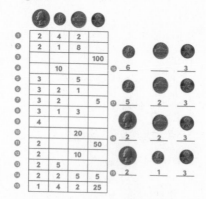

Answer order may vary between
numbers 1–15.

Page 36
Answer: **MEET YOU AT NOON!**

Page 37
The actual measurements will vary
somewhat, but they should be
close to the following:
1. 14 1/2 inches 2. 19 inches
3. 13 1/2 inches 4. 21 inches

Page 38
Answers will vary.

Page 39
1. ounces 2. pounds 3. ounces
4. pounds 5. pounds 6. pounds
7. ounces 8. ounces 9. pounds
10. ounces 11. ounces 12. pounds
13. pounds 14. ounces 15. ounces

Page 40
1. 90˚F 2. 0˚C 3. 30˚C 4. 55˚F
5. 30˚F 6. 40˚F 7. 68˚F 8. 20˚C
9. 75˚F 10. 80˚F

Page 41
1. 100 2. 7 3. 36 4. 365 5. 60
6. 12 7. 12 8. 4 9. 26 10. 20
11. 16 12. 52 13. 5 14. 2 15. 24

Page 42
1. 5 2. 11 3. 30 4. 16 5. 8 6. 17

Page 43
1. G 2. B 3. C or A 4. I 5. E 6. C 7. F
8. I 9. F 10. E 11. I 12. F 13. I 14. C
15. C 16. C 17. G 18. C 19. F 20. B

Page 44

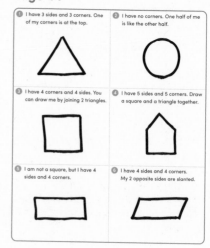

Pages 45–46
Tessellation patterns will vary.